"THESE GUYS"

Should We Be Afraid?

Kevin Simmons' Theory

Table Of Contents

Introduction

When you ask people what they're afraid of, a few common answers pop up: public speaking, needles, global warming, losing a loved one. But if you take a look at popular media, you would think we were all terrified of sharks, dolls, and clowns.

While the last item may give a few people pause, 7.8 percent of Americans totally get it, according to a Chapman University survey.

A fear of clowns, called coulrophobia (pronounced "coal-ruh-fow-bee-uh"), can be a debilitating fear.A phobia is an intense fear of a certain object or scenario that impacts behavior and sometimes daily life. Phobias are often a deep-rooted psychological response tied to a traumatic event in someone's past.

For people who fear clowns, it can be difficult to stay calm near events that others view with joy — circuses, carnivals, or other festivals. The good news is you're not alone, and there are things you can do to ease your fears.

Chapter One
The History And Psychology

There's a word— albeit one not recognized by the Oxford English Dictionary or any psychology manual— for the excessive fear of clowns: Coulrophobia.

Not a lot of people actually suffer from a debilitating phobia of clowns; a lot more people, however, just don't like them.

In Sarasota, Florida, in 2006, communal loathing for clowns took a criminal turn when dozens of fiberglass clown statues—part of a public art exhibition called "Clowning Around Town" and a nod to the city's history as a winter haven for traveling circuses—were defaced, their limbs broken, heads lopped off, spray-painted; two were abducted and we can only guess at their sad fates. Even the people who are supposed to like clowns—children—supposedly don't. In 2008, a widely reported University of Sheffield, England, survey of 250 children between the ages of four and 16 found that most of the children disliked and even feared images of clowns. The BBC's report on the study featured a child psychologist who broadly declared, "Very few children like clowns. They are unfamiliar and come from a different era. They don't look funny, they just look odd." But most clowns aren't trying to be odd. They're trying to be silly and sweet, fun personified. So the question is, when did the clown, supposedly a jolly figure of innocuous, kid-friendly entertainment, become so weighed down by fear and sadness? When did clowns become so dark?

Maybe they always have been.

Clowns, as pranksters, jesters, jokers, harlequins, and mythologized tricksters have been around for ages. They appear in most cultures—Pygmy clowns made Egyptian pharaohs laugh in 2500 BCE; in ancient imperial China, a court clown called YuSze was, according to the lore, the only guy who could poke holes in Emperor Qin Shih Huang's plan to paint the Great Wall of China; Hopi Native Americans had a tradition of clown-like characters who interrupted serious dance rituals with ludicrous antics. Ancient Rome's clown was a stock fool called the stupidus; the court jesters of medieval Europe were a sanctioned way for people under the feudal thumb to laugh at the guys in charge; and well into the 18th and 19th century, the prevailing clown figure of Western Europe and Britain was the pantomime clown, who was a sort of bumbling buffoon. But clowns have always had a dark side, says David Kiser, director of talent for Ringling Bros. and Barnum & Bailey Circus. After all, these were characters who reflected a funhouse mirror back on society; academics note that their comedy was often derived from their voracious appetites for food, sex, and drink, and their manic behavior. "So in one way, the clown has always been an impish spirit… as he's kind of grown up, he's always been about fun, but part of that fun has been a bit of mischief," says Kiser.

Mischief" is one thing; homicidal urges are certainly another. What's changed about clowns is how that darkness is manifest, argued Andrew McConnell Stott, Dean of Undergraduate Education and an English professor at the University of Buffalo, SUNY.
Clowns were comic relief from the thrills and chills of the daring circus acts, an anarchic presence that complimented the precision of the acrobats or horse riders. At the same time, their humor necessarily became broader—the clowns had more space to fill, so their movements and actions needed to be more obvious.

Chapter Two

The Four Types Of Clowns

We recognize them all: the clown with the pretty white face and the almost aristocratic bearing; the tramp with his bindle ("blanket stick"), so sad, never catching a break; the everyman with the oversize shoes, who trips and causes the man on the ladder to fall into a tub of water and finally,the impersonator.

We enjoy their antics, but we may never have noticed that all clowns can be traced back to one of these four clown types: the Whiteface, the Tramp,the Auguste (or 'fool') and the Character clown. Each type has its own history, its own set of clown characteristics, and a typical look.

The Whiteface Clown

The oldest of all clowns, the Whiteface can be traced back through commedia dell'arte and medieval court jesters to the theaters of ancient Greece, where comedic actors frequently painted their features white so they could be better seen.The Whiteface is the big brother of the clowning world: in charge, a know-it-all, a straight man setting up the situations that other clowns, like the Auguste or the Tramp, turn funny. The customary features of the Whiteface include a full white face, red-and-white features (often quite beautiful and delicate), a colorful outfit, and a wig.

The Whiteface can be further divided into three groups: The Classic (European) Whiteface, sometimes called the 'most majestic and beautiful' of the Whitefaces; an elegant clown, like the Pierrot or Harlequin of commedia dell'arte;

The Straight Whiteface, similar to the Classic but more colorful, more cheerful; and

The Grotesque Whiteface, similar to the Straight Whiteface in color and cheer, but zanier, with exaggerated features and clothes.
The Mime, also an elegant clown, known of course for not speaking but emoting through body language and facial expressions.

Famous Whiteface clowns include Frosty Little, Bozo the Clown and Ronald McDonald.

The Auguste Clown

The Auguste (pronounced ah-GOOST) is a mixture of Whiteface and Tramp — not so hapless as the Tramp, but wilder and broader than the Whiteface. He is sometimes the Whiteface's helper, almost always the brunt of his jokes, and certain to mess up any assignment.

The classic Auguste appearance is the opposite of the
Whiteface, with prominent fleshtones and
black-and-white features, a large ball-shaped nose, and
extravagant mismatched costumes (oversized neckties,
very small hats, etc.).

A common variation on the Auguste is the
Contra-Auguste, sometimes described as an Auguste
trying to be a Whiteface. He mediates the conflict
between the Whiteface and the Auguste, often with
funny results.
Famous Augustes include Cookie (from the Bozo Show)
and Coco.

The Tramp Clown

A uniquely American clown, some believe that the idea
of the Tramp originated with the hobos who rode the
rails during the Great Depression. The classic Tramp
look a sooty face, with white around the eyes and mouth
may refer back to the coal smoke from America's rail
yards.

The Tramp is the brunt of every joke, the one whose
rear gets kicked, the one whose face gets wet from a
squirting flower. The customary features of the Tramp
include a flesh-toned face, a beard of stubble, a ruddy
nose, tattered suit and hat, and fingerless gloves.
The Tramp can be further divided into three groups,
though the basic costume remains the same for each:

- The Classic Tramp, forlorn and downtrodden, shuffling through life with a rain cloud over his head;

-

- The Hobo or Vagabond, his manners are often elegant and refined; he's happy to be free of society; and

-

- The Bag Lady, a female version of the Tramp or Hobo

-

Tramps have been made famous by such luminaries as Charlie Chaplin, Emmett Kelly, and Red Skelton.

Character Clown

Whilst most clowns are fairly generic in their appearance a character clown has a very specific and clearly recognisable identity. Charlie Chaplin could be classed as a character clown. The little tramp with his funny walk and cane became very famous in the days of the silent movie. Another very well known character clown was Emmet Kelly. He was an American circus clown who was always sad.Character clowns often mimic a respectable profession. They are poking fun at the establishment which is why people find them amusing. The bungling policeman, an absent minded headmaster, a silly doctor all have great potential for this role.Character clowns can be employed to great effect at events. It's great fun to have a clown policeman at the entrance in charge of security. The absent minded headmaster is a good one for educational / school events. Clown doctors often work in hospitals. A cowboy clown is great for a wild west themed event.

Chapter Three
The People's View

Coulrophobia is no laughing matter. This irrational fear of clowns can cause panic and nausea. Although it's a rare phobia, many people find clowns creepy if not downright scary. Why? The answer lies partly in the prevalence of evil clowns in popular culture—think Pennywise in Stephen King's It (1986). However, according to researchers, there are actual psychological reasons why we fear clowns.

To begin with, a clown's makeup can be unsettling. It hides not only the person's identity but also that person's feelings. Worse, the makeup can result in mixed signals if, for example, the clown has a painted-on smile but is frowning. Then, there's the uncanny nature of the makeup itself. The oversized lips and eyebrows distort the face so that the brain perceives it as human but slightly off. That oddness is heightened by a clown's bizarre costume. In addition, clowns are highly unpredictable as well as mischievous, which puts people on edge. Are they going to squirt water at you or give you a flower?

These psychological discomforts produce a fear that is then stoked by negative portrayals of clowns in popular culture. According to some, 1970s American serial killer John Wayne Gacy—who performed as Pogo the Clown at charity events and children's parties—solidified the idea of the evil clown, and that trope became common in horror movies and books. So perhaps it's not surprising that a 2016 poll found that Americans were more afraid of clowns than of a terrorist attack or even dying.

A clown going around killing people is the stuff of nightmares, so it's no surprise that John Wayne Gacy and his heinous crimes still have the power to shock and appall.

The former KFC manager killed 33 men in the 1970s, and also moonlighted as a clown, called Pogo or Patches, performing at local charity events, parades, store openings and hospitals to entertain sick children. Pogo's make-up was a plain white face, oversized red lips and big blue beehive-shaped eyes.

In 1992 he spoke to an FBI investigator about how he found wearing the circus garb "relaxing".

During July 1975, a teenager who worked for Gacy disappeared. His parent's pleaded with Chicago police officers to investigate Gacy, but they never did. This would not be the last time worried parents asked officials to review Gacy as a suspect, but the pleas fell on deaf ears. In 1976, Gacy divorced for a second time, and it seemed to give him a feeling of personal freedom. Unknown to anyone else at the time, Gacy began to rape and kill young men. Over a period of just a few years, he murdered 33 people, 29 of whom were found underneath Gacy's house — 26 in the crawlspace and 3 other bodies were found in other areas beneath his home.

A young man went to the Chicago police for help in 1977, claiming that he had been kidnapped and molested by John Wayne Gacy. A report was made, but officers failed to follow up on it. The following year, Gacy murdered a 15-year-old boy who had gone to Gacy's home to ask about a job with his construction company. This time, the Des Plaines police got involved and searched Gacy's home. They found a class ring, clothing for much smaller individuals, and other suspicious items. Upon further investigation, officers discovered that the ring belonged to a teenage boy who was missing, and they found a witness who claimed Gacy had admitted to killing up to 30 people.

Chapter Four

Their Secret Lives

More than one million people saw Cirque du Soleil's Corteo with Jeff Raz in the starring role. Every night after the show, Raz hurried back to the hotel to do his "day job" as the director of the only school for professional clowns in the United States. The Secret Life of Clowns was born from Raz's attempts to take the principles he taught at The Clown Conservatory into the grand chapiteau in front of 2,800 Cirque du Soleil fans eight times a week. The form of the book is modeled on Constantin Stanislavski's brilliant trilogy that brought the Moscow Art Theater to the world through the eyes of a fictionalized student. Since Raz was simultaneously running a school and starring in a show, he has doubled up on Stanislavski with twin narratives - a fictionalized Clown Conservatory and a backstage tour of Cirque du Soleil.

Some artists thrive by taking risks, exploring unknown territory, living on the edge. The title character in The Snow Clown takes this literally, flying tiny planes out to Eskimo villages in the dead of winter to teach kids who have never seen a circus. The unforgiving tundra and triple-digit wind chill are the least of his worries as he navigates a world where traditional Yup'ik culture is fighting off TV America and missionary teachers.

Years later, the Snow Clown finds himself in Nebraska, America's Heartland, performing a comedy about the

Holocaust and his father's suicide. It doesn't go well. He
is a Jewish artist out on the plains where Jews are as
rare as buffalo but burning crosses are not. Using skills
he honed on the Alaskan tundra, he writes plays with
students that blow the lid off of "Nebraska Nice" and
eventually get him run out of town.
Frank Singer gets the call he's been waiting for his
whole career, an invitation to fly to Europe and star in
the best-loved circus on earth. But he can't say "yes."
His circus family - strong, independent, wildly creative
people - need him at home like they never have before.
As high-flying as they are on stage, literally and
figuratively, Frank's community comes right down to
earth when people start dying.

Chapter Five
Dealing With Coulrophobia

Who is at Risk?
Coulrophobia affects all ages and genders, although females may be more likely to be afraid of clowns. Researchers have noted signs of coulrophobia in children as young as 3. You may be more at risk for developing this specific phobic disorder if you already have an anxiety disorder or other phobias.

What Are The Causes?
People with coulrophobia may be reacting to a clown's colorful makeup. This disguise hides a clown's facial features and distorts facial expressions, creating feelings of distrust.

What Are The Symptoms?
Children and adults with coulrophobia may try to get away from a clown, hide behind a person or object, or cover their eyes so that they don't have to see the clown. A child may cry. Sometimes, just the possibility of seeing a clown causes an anxious response.

Other signs of coulrophobia include:
- Fast breathing and heart rate.
- An intense feeling of terror.

- Pale skin.
- Profuse sweating (hyperhidrosis).
- Nausea.
- Trembling or shaking.

How Is It Diagnosed?

The American Psychiatric Association (APA) doesn't recognize coulrophobia as a phobic disorder in its Diagnostic and Statistical Manual of Mental Disorders (DSM). There are no set criteria for diagnosing it.

A healthcare provider may recommend an evaluation with a mental health professional like a psychologist. This provider may diagnose coulrophobia after evaluating symptoms, including the impact of the phobia on daily life.

You or your child may have a specific phobic disorder like coulrophobia if the fear:

- Occurs when you see a clown or its image.
- Causes you to avoid certain situations like parties or the movies.
- Brings on intense distress that doesn't match the actual danger.
- Lasts six months or longer.
- Affects your quality of life.

Management And Treatment

There isn't a specific coulrophobia treatment. If the phobia disrupts your quality of life, exposure therapy with a mental health professional may help. Exposure therapy is a type of psychotherapy or talk therapy. It can help as many as 9 in 10 people overcome specific phobias.

Exposure therapy involves gradual and repeated exposures to images or situations that trigger coulrophobia symptoms. The process involves:
Learning breathing and relaxation techniques to use before and during exposure.
Viewing images or videos of clowns. (A child may benefit from watching a person put on clown makeup and transform into a clown.)
Gradually progressing to being in the same area as a clown.
Eventually, being next to a clown or holding and viewing a clown image.

Conclusion

Many children and adults express a fear of clowns. People with coulrophobia go out of their way to avoid any exposure to clowns or clown images. Fortunately, running into clowns isn't a typical, everyday occurrence. You or your child can take steps to avoid seeing clowns and clown images. If the fear becomes too great, don't hesitate to talk to your healthcare provider. Exposure therapy with a mental health professional can help you manage this phobia.